Summary

What drives governments to crack down on and kill their own civilians? And how—and to what extent—has nonviolent resistance mitigated the likelihood of mass killings? This special report explores the factors associated with mass killings: when governments intentionally kill 1,000 or more civilian noncombatants. We find that these events are surprisingly common, occurring in just under half of maximalist popular uprisings against the states, yet they are strongly associated with certain types of resistance. Specifically, we find that:

- Nonviolent resistance is generally less threatening to the physical well-being of regime elites, lowering the odds of mass killings. This is true even though these campaigns may take place in repressive contexts, demand that political leaders share power or step aside, and are historically quite successful at toppling brutal regimes.
- Violent campaigns that threaten the safety of incumbent leaders, however, might inspire them to hold on to power at any cost, leading to mass atrocities as a last resort.
- Leaders who order their armed forces to crack down on unarmed civilians run the risk of defection and insubordination. The possibility of losing this crucial pillar of support might deter leaders from launching mass atrocities in the first place.
- The likelihood of mass killings is greater when foreign states provide material aid to dissidents. Violent insurgencies often rely on this assistance to generate money and accumulate weapons that are necessary to confront the regime. Nonviolent campaigns, however, can partner with non-governmental organizations that provide less overt forms of support. This might include knowledge-sharing and capacity-building efforts that yield more effective grassroots mobilization and repression management.

Taken together, these findings shed light on how dissidents, their allies, and the international community can work together to reduce the likelihood of mass killings.

About the authors

 **Evan Perkoski** is an assistant professor in the Department of Political Science at the University of Connecticut. His research focuses on the dynamics of rebel, insurgent, and terrorist groups; strategies of violent and nonviolent resistance; and the behavior of state and nonstate actors in cyberspace. His book manuscript explores the breakdown of armed organizations, focusing particularly on the emergence of splinter groups and how they behave relative to their predecessors. He received his PhD from the University of Pennsylvania and has held fellowships at the Belfer Center for Science and International Affairs at the Harvard Kennedy School of Government as well as the Josef Korbel School of International Studies at the University of Denver.

 **Erica Chenoweth** is a professor at the Josef Korbel School of International Studies at the University of Denver. *Foreign Policy* magazine ranked her among the Top 100 Global Thinkers of 2013 for her work to advance the empirical study of civil resistance. Her book, *Why Civil Resistance Works* (Columbia University Press, 2011) with Maria J. Stephan, also won the 2013 Grawemeyer Award for Ideas Improving World Order. Chenoweth has authored or edited four books and dozens of articles on political violence and its alternatives. She earned a PhD and an MA from the University of Colorado and a BA from the University of Dayton.

Table of contents

Summary	2
About the authors	3
Introduction	5
When and where mass killings occur	7
Why do mass killings occur? Common structural explanations	12
Why do mass killings occur? Unique campaign-level explanations	14
Main findings: Why do mass killings occur?	16
I. Structural and elite-driven factors	16
II. Campaign-level factors	18
III. Assessing campaign and structural factors: which matter more?	20
Key takeaways	22
For dissidents	23
For foreign states, policymakers, and NGOs	24
Future research	26
End Notes	27

Tables and figures

Figure 1: Mass killings in violent and nonviolent campaigns	8
Figure 2: The geographic distribution of mass killings	9
Figure 3: Mass killings over time	10
Figure 4: Violent and nonviolent campaigns, 1945-2013	11
Figure 5: Top 10 predictors impacting odds of mass killings	21

Case studies

Key definitions	7
Escalatory violence and mass killings in Central African Republic	13
Mass killings in Biafra	17
Civil resistance in Serbia	20
Top 10 prediction-improving variables	21
Mass killings in Syria and the evolving campaign of resistance	22

Introduction

Between 1950 and 2013, mass killings occurred in almost 43% of popular uprisings that challenged incumbent regimes. These campaigns either sought to overthrow and replace the existing government or to fundamentally reshape their political institutions. Yet, as this also implies, a significant proportion of uprisings did not experience a mass killing. In a majority of cases—57%—dissidents were spared from the brutal violence that befell many of their counterparts in other countries. Why, then, do some dissidents face less direct state violence than others? Relying on newly collected data and original analysis, this special report aims to shed light on the factors that increase or decrease the odds of government-led mass killings during popular resistance campaigns.

Popular uprisings are not all alike. Some, like those in Libya (2011) and eventually Syria (2011), are predominantly violent, wherein the opposition chooses to take up arms to challenge the status quo. Others, like Tunisia (2010), Egypt (2011), and Burkina Faso (2014) eschew violence altogether, challenging the regime through a plethora of largely nonviolent actions (Sharp 1973; Schock 2005; Chenoweth and Stephan 2011). In this report we focus our attention on these and other overlooked campaign characteristics—such as their method of resistance, whether they have foreign support, and what exactly they seek to achieve—to shed light on how governments respond differently based on characteristics of the uprising itself. In doing so we move beyond a typical focus on structural factors like poverty, ethnic fractionalizaton, and institutionalized discrimination to explain regime violence toward civilians. Our research suggests that the strategic interaction between dissidents and regimes is central to the occurrence of mass violence and that characteristics of these campaigns play a significant role in explaining the likelihood of mass atrocities.

The main finding of this report is that nonviolent uprisings are almost three times less likely than violent rebellions to encounter mass killings, all else being equal. There are several explanations:

- Nonviolent resistance is generally less threatening to the physical well-being of regime elites, lowering the odds of violent retaliation. This is true even though these campaigns may take place in repressive contexts, demand that political leaders share power or step aside, and are historically quite successful at toppling brutal regimes.
- Violent campaigns that threaten the safety of incumbent leaders, however, might inspire them to hold on to power at any cost, leading to mass atrocities as a perceived last resort.
- Leaders who order their armed forces to crack down on unarmed civilians run the risk of defection and insubordination. The possibility of losing this crucial pillar of support might deter leaders from launching mass atrocities in the first place.
- Finally, the likelihood of mass killings is greater when foreign states provide material aid to dissidents. Violent insurgencies often rely on this assistance to generate money and accumulate weapons that are necessary to confront the regime. Nonviolent campaigns, however, can partner with non-governmental organizations that provide less overt forms of support. This might include knowledge-sharing and capacity-building efforts that yield more effective grassroots mobilization and repression management.

Nonviolent movements, then, have a number of comparative advantages that ultimately decrease the odds of inciting intense and direct government violence.

In this report we survey existing explanations for mass killings, theorize how dissidents might impact the government's strategic calculus regarding the use of force, and briefly explain our methodology for studying these events. Ultimately, we find that a host of factors influences the timing of mass killings. Some of these are associated with the nature of violent and nonviolent campaigns while others capture important aspects both of the government and the country at large. While this implies that the decision to commit mass atrocities is partly a function of the structural environment, it shows how the actions and strategies of dissidents—particularly the decision to challenge the regime without arms—are influential as well, and their agency should not be overlooked. We conclude the report by offering specific and general recommendations for various constituents to both reduce mass violence and increase the safety of those struggling for meaningful political change.

> **Box 1: Key definitions**
>
> **Mass Killings** are the intentional killing of 1,000 or more civilian noncombatants by government-led or directed forces in a sustained, continuous event. We use the terms "mass killing," "mass atrocities," and "mass violence" interchangeably.
>
> **Uprisings** are observable, continuous, coordinated, purposive mass events in pursuit of a political objective through either violent or nonviolent means. We use the terms "campaigns," "uprisings," "popular uprisings," "contentious episodes" and "struggles" interchangeably.
>
> **Nonviolent Resistance** refers to civilian uprisings where the dominant method of resistance eschews directly and physically harming others. This might involve protests, sit-ins, walk-outs, or other coordinated, purposive events that deliberately avoid violent confrontations. We use the term "nonviolent resistance" interchangeably with "nonviolent uprisings," "civil resistance," "nonviolent campaigns," "nonviolent struggles," and "nonviolent conflict."
>
> **Maximalist Claim** refers to a demand that would fundamentally reshape the central political regime of a country through the overthrow of an incumbent national leader, territorial secession, independence from colonial power, or the expulsion of a foreign military occupation.

When and where mass killings occur

The focus of our study is mass killings, which are intentional killings of 1,000 or more civilian noncombatants by government-led or directed forces in a sustained, continuous event. In other words, these are events where incumbent regimes use widespread force against their own populations, killings thousands, if not many more, in the process. Importantly, this definition notes that mass killings can be carried out by government-led or directed forces. In many cases, such as the genocide in Rwanda, it is not only the state's formal military that launches violent operations but local militias and other organizations participate as well. This definition also makes it clear that the targets of violence are civilian noncombatants and not soldiers or other rebel groups in an ongoing civil war.

Relying on data from 1955 to 2013,[1] we find that mass killings commonly occur in the context of popular uprisings. Among the 308 violent and nonviolent campaigns we identify,[2] 132 experienced a mass killing while 176 did not. In other words, 43% of uprisings, regardless of their method of resistance, encounter mass violence at some point during the campaign. Thus, the odds that resisters are met with mass, lethal violence is close to a coin flip.

Looking within campaigns, however, we find meaningful variation suggesting that not all uprisings are equally likely to encounter mass atrocities. Figure 1A, below, depicts the proportion of violent uprisings that experience mass killings, and Figure 1B plots the proportion of nonviolent uprisings that experience mass killings. As these figures show, violent uprisings are nearly three times as likely to elicit state violence. Specifically, nearly 68% of violent uprisings (92 of 135 campaigns) encounter mass killings while it is closer to 23% (40 of 173 campaigns) for predominantly nonviolent movements. Thus, while nearly 43% of all uprisings experience a mass atrocity, many more of these events occur in the context of violent, rather than nonviolent, opposition to the state.

This imbalance in personal safety that favors nonviolent activists is echoed in other research as well. A separate ICNC Monograph by Jonathan Pinckney finds that governments repress individual acts of nonviolent resistance at a much lower rate than violent resistance.[3] While nonviolent acts lead to repression 12% of the time, it is over 70% for purely violent or "mixed" events. Taken together, this provides preliminary evidence that nonviolent strategies seem to be relatively safer for individual activists.

Figure 1: Mass killings in violent and nonviolent campaigns

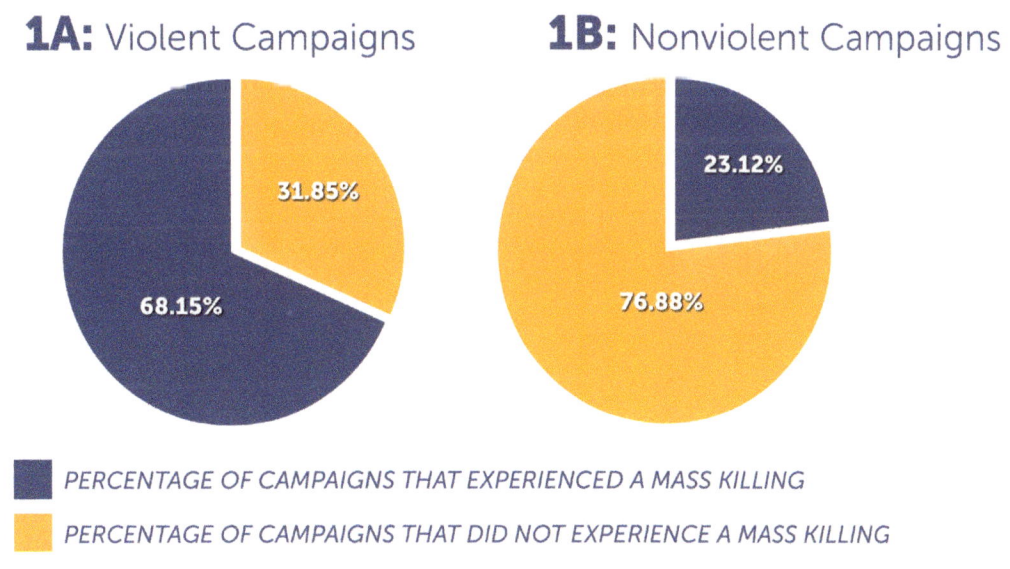

1A: Violent Campaigns — 68.15% / 31.85%
1B: Nonviolent Campaigns — 23.12% / 76.88%

PERCENTAGE OF CAMPAIGNS THAT EXPERIENCED A MASS KILLING
PERCENTAGE OF CAMPAIGNS THAT DID NOT EXPERIENCE A MASS KILLING

There is also meaningful variation in the occurrence of mass killings across space and time. The greatest proportion of such events are concentrated in Africa (39 campaigns with mass killings since 1955, or 29.55%) followed by East Asia and the Pacific (26 or 19.7%), and then South and Central Asia (21 or 15.91%). See Figure 2 on next page.

Figure 2: The geographic distribution of mass killings

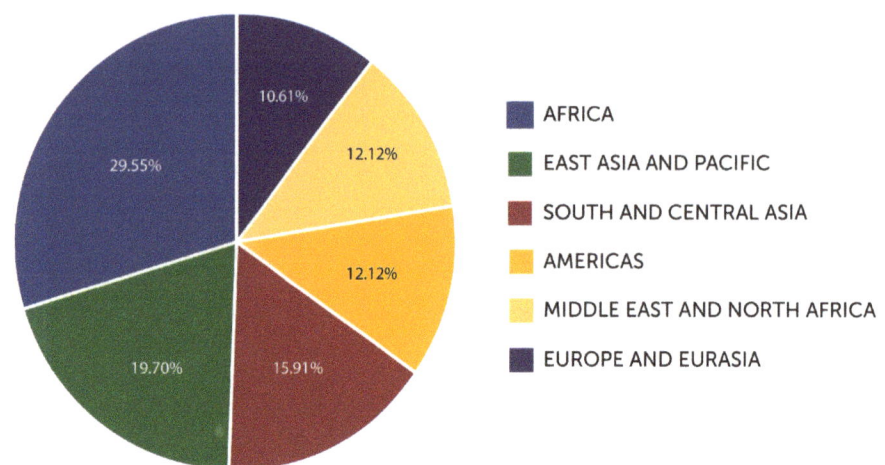

With regard to variation over time, mass killings seem to have peaked in the early 1990s, particularly in 1992 when 36 new or ongoing mass killings took place. Although these events have been steadily on the rise since 1955, this trend began to reverse after 1992. Since then, mass killings have declined to some of their lowest observed levels. In 2010, for instance, there were 11 ongoing mass killings, occurring in Colombia, Congo-Kinshasa, India, Indonesia, Iran, Laos, Nigeria, North Korea, Philippines, Uganda, and Vietnam. In 2013 the number rose to 15 with new mass killings occurring in Central African Republic, Egypt, South Sudan, Sudan, and Syria, and mass violence ending in India. See Figure 3 on the next page for the frequency of and decline in mass killings over the last two decades.

Figure 3: Mass killings over time

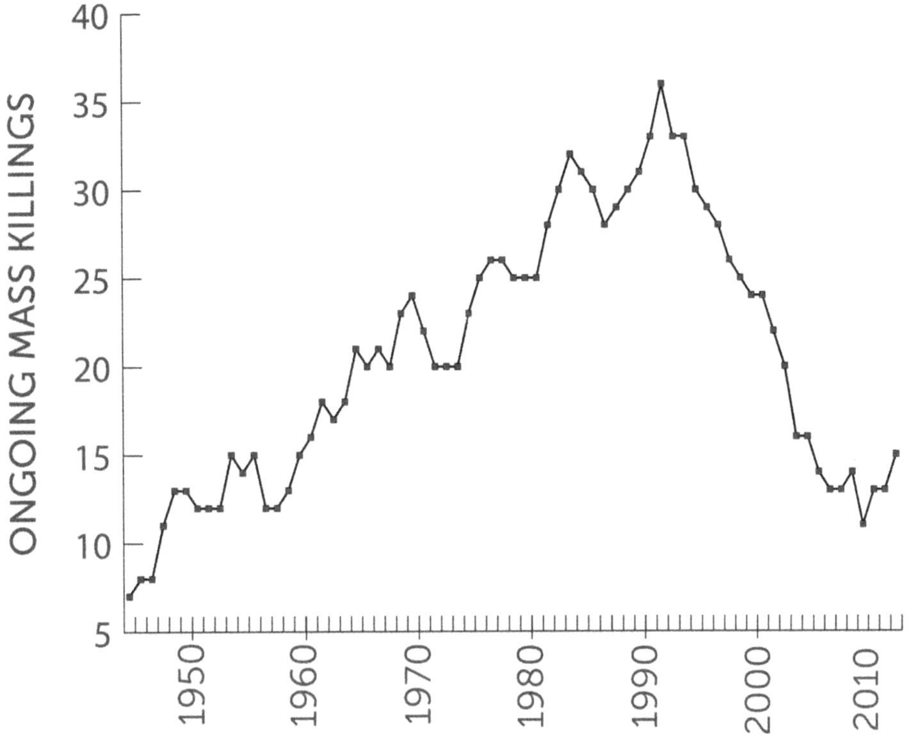

Mass killings peaked in 1992, taking place in 36 countries: Afghanistan, Algeria, Angola, Azerbaijan, Bangladesh, Bosnia and Herzegovina, Burundi, Chad, Colombia, Congo-Brazzaville, El Salvador, Georgia, Guatemala, Haiti, India, Indonesia, Iran, Iraq, Laos, Malawi, Mozambique, Nigeria, North Korea, Papua New Guinea, Peru, Philippines, Rwanda, Sierra Leone, South Africa, Sri Lanka, Sudan, Tajikistan, Turkey, Uganda, Vietnam, and Yugoslavia.

There are several plausible explanations for the observed decline in mass killings in the last 25 years: perhaps most significantly, nonviolent resistance campaigns have become more common, whereas violent insurgencies have steadily declined since the end of the Cold War (see Figure 4 on the next page). Additionally, the ubiquity of internet-connected devices has made it harder for regimes to conceal mass atrocities, increasing the likelihood of both domestic and international condemnation. Finally, the evolving web of international human rights norms, including the Responsibility to Protect, might play a role. Despite how inconsistently they are applied, these widely accepted norms might have a socializing and deterrent effect on states thinking about using violence against their own civilians. Nonetheless, additional research is required to fully understand the factors contributing to the worldwide decline of mass killings.

Figure 4: Violent and nonviolent campaigns, 1945-2013

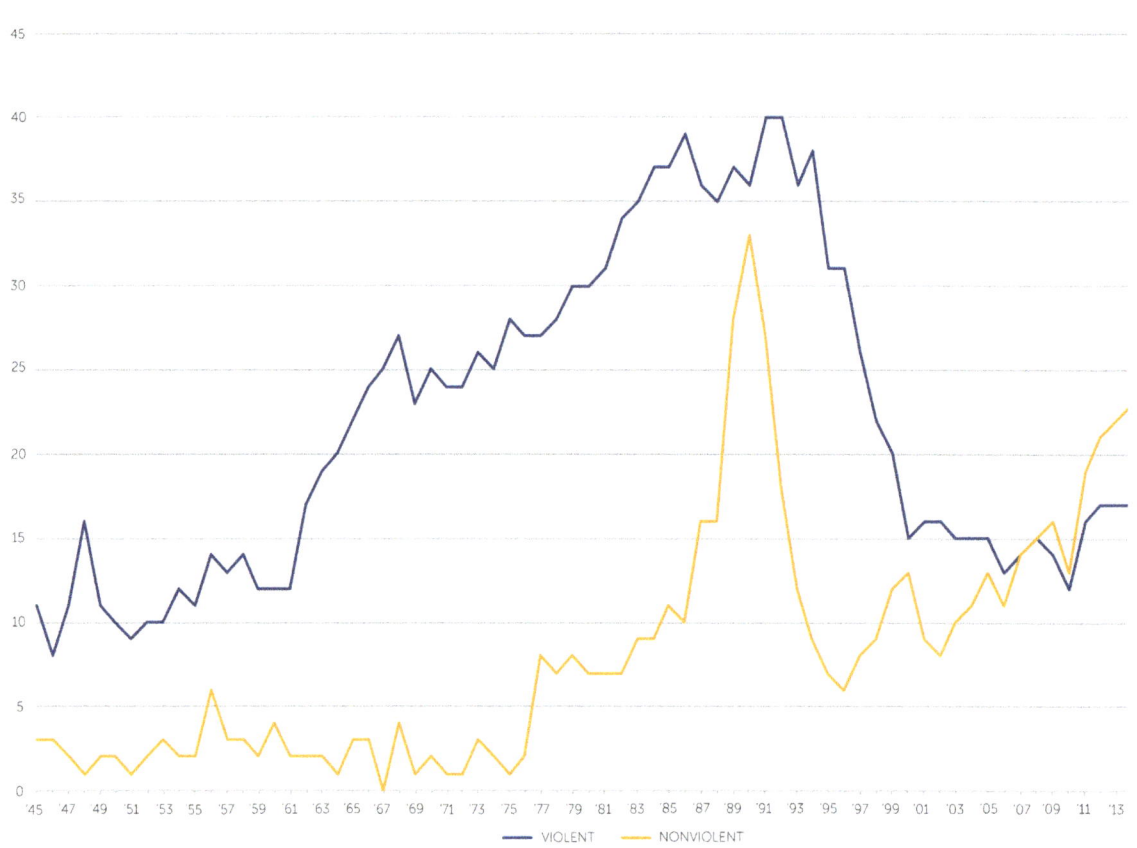

Source: https://www.du.edu/korbel/sie/research/chenow_navco_data.html

Why do mass killings occur? Common structural explanations

Existing studies commonly focus on two factors to explain mass killings: capacity and threat.[4] With regard to the first factor, states require a minimum military capability to successfully coordinate and carry out mass killings. Military campaigns to kill such large numbers of people require not only coordination, but also sufficient control, training, and resources. Nonstate actors, therefore, will likely find the resources and logistical challenges more daunting, which might explain why states more commonly perpetrate such acts. With regard to the second factor, threat, research suggests that mass killings are especially likely when regime elites face existential threats to their continued survival and rule.[5] This is particularly likely when states are countering insurgent movements that derive resources and support from the local population: states may use mass killings to deter civilians from further supporting the rebels. Mass violence in counterinsurgency efforts, then, is a way that states try to influence civilian populations in order to gain a military advantage.[6]

Thus, the common understanding of mass killings is that they are essentially last-ditch efforts by capable regimes to maintain power and preserve the status quo. It is only when a regime is faced with an imminent threat to its survival, coupled with sufficient military capacity, that scholars expect mass killings to take place. In such circumstances, capable leaders may view mass killings as a means to quell domestic unrest, defeat a growing insurgency, and maintain their grip on power. Viewed in this way, mass killings are highly intentional, rational acts that have a strategic purpose.[7]

> ## Box 2: Escalatory violence and mass killings in Central African Republic
>
> Mass violence in Central African Republic began soon after an alliance of predominantly Muslim rebel groups, going by the name Seleka (literally meaning "alliance"), seized power from the Christian coalition headed by General François Bozizé, the incumbent of nearly 10 years. Soon after his downfall, Christian militias began to organize in response to sporadic yet organized violence from rogue Seleka commanders and fighters. This, in turn, precipitated a spiral of violence as Christian militias retaliated against Muslim populations. The violence in Central African Republic illustrates many of the factors commonly associated with the onset of mass killings including a violent uprising, foreign involvement, subgroup discrimination, and an authoritarian regime type.
>
> Source: Human Rights Watch, "'They Came To Kill' Escalating Atrocities in the Central African Republic." https://www.hrw.org/report/2013/12/18/they-came-kill/escalating-atrocities-central-african-republic

In studying threat and capacity, researchers often focus on structural factors, or characteristics of a state and its ruling regime. This often includes regime type and power concentration, ethnic fractionalization, GDP per capita, and level of development. These slow-moving structural indicators, however, provide little insight into the timing of mass killing outbreaks. Based on these factors alone, many countries could be considered at an elevated risk for mass atrocities, obscuring cases of imminent violence. Moreover, because they are difficult to influence in the short term, structural factors provide policy makers and outside actors with few options to prevent or forestall mass killings once they seem likely to occur. Taken together, insights from structural factors alone make it difficult for policymakers and external actors to effectively focus and direct their prevention efforts.

Perhaps more significantly, structural factors do not help us understand the timing of mass atrocities. GDP, development metrics, and regime type, for instance, tend to be relatively constant from one year to the next, usually changing in small, predictable ways. Based solely on these factors, however, a country may be considered at risk for decades, leaving policymakers with little sense of urgency even though a mass atrocity might be imminent. Structural factors therefore give us little insight into when civilians in a country are most likely to encounter violence.

Existing studies of mass killings also tend to focus on large-scale internal wars as the predominant threat to a state, often looking exclusively at civil wars and major insurgencies. We know less about the dynamics of conflicts not yet reaching these thresholds, and we know almost nothing about how nonviolent uprisings compare to violent ones as far as mass killings are concerned. Recent events, and particularly the Arab Spring, demonstrate that dictators sometimes fall and sometimes crack down on their populations in response to nonviolent movements, suggesting that we should broaden the scope of cases in which the international community must prioritize the prevention of mass killings.

Why do mass killings occur? Unique campaign-level explanations

Our research, and this report, differ from most existing studies of mass killings by exploring how numerous characteristics of contentious episodes shape the likelihood of massive state violence. These campaign-level factors include:

a) The primary mode of contention (nonviolent or violent);
b) The dissidents' goals (what they are seeking to achieve);
c) The behavior of repressive agents (e.g. defections from the armed forces); and
d) External interventions supporting the dissidents, the regime, or both.

Ultimately, we argue that regimes will not necessarily view all uprisings as equally threatening. Rather, some—like large-scale, foreign-backed, violent rebellions seeking to overthrow and replace the incumbent regime—are much more likely to trigger mass violence. On the other hand, predominantly nonviolent uprisings—where incumbent political leaders can potentially abandon their posts without fear of personal harm—should experience mass killings at a much lower rate. It might also be easier to negotiate an end to nonviolent uprisings since the "sunk costs" in terms of mobilization, lives lost, and destroyed property are generally lower than in violent rebellions. This option might give regime elites a credible way out that avoids mass killings.

In addition, extant research finds that civilian victimization often occurs in disputed territories (Kalyvas 2006, Kaplan 2017), which is common in violent rebellions where strategically-valuable territory is a desirable commodity. On the other hand, civil resistance campaigns, even those aiming to remove unwanted powerholders, are more concerned with battles for legitimacy than battles for territory (Ackerman and DuVall 2001), which might further lower the odds of mass violence.

Finally, in cases where leaders do order violence against nonviolent protesters, we expect to witness high rates of defection from the armed forces. The fear of defection during a nonviolent uprising could in fact lead regime elites to refrain from using violence in the first place. Moreover, the fact that nonviolent struggles, on average, either succeed or fail three times faster than their violent counterparts (Chenoweth and Stephan 2011) significantly reduces the time period in which mass killings might occur. Long, drawn-out conflicts, however, might incentivize regime elites to utilize mass killings to break the stalemate.

We analyze the available data[8] in two stages: first, we run traditional correlation analyses (logistics regressions) to understand which factors are associated with mass killings in the context of popular uprisings. Second, we employ statistical forecasting techniques (specifically, out-of-sample validation) to better understand which factors are the best predictors of mass killings.[9] To do this, we divide our data in two: from 1970 to 1999 (the training set) and from 2000 to 2013 (the validation set). Then, after running regression models and obtaining coefficient estimates from the training set, we see how well these same models predict instances of mass killings in the validation set.[10] This method has a number of benefits, but perhaps most significantly, the results give us a sense of how well the model can not only explain past mass killings, but also how well it accurately predicts more recent mass killings.[11]

Main findings: Why do mass killings occur?

I. Structural and elite-driven factors: regime type; leaders' tenure; state discrimination; poverty; size of the population; military takeovers; recent mass killings

First, our analysis of the structural variables associated with mass killings confirms the same patterns identified by other researchers.[12] We find that regime type matters, and specifically, military and party-based authoritarian regimes are more likely than others to commit a mass killing. It could be that these regime types exhibit especially strong internal cohesion, military control, and capability, allowing them to order and carry out a mass killing with little fear of defection. Similarly, a leader's tenure in office is also correlated with mass killings. Leaders with long, uninterrupted holds on power might be particularly reluctant to accede to protesters' demands, opting instead to use force to maintain their office. Indeed, this calls to mind many dictators like Bashar Al-Assad, Hosni Mubarak, Muammar Gaddafi, and others who utilized violence in an attempt to shore up their regime and maintain power in the face of widespread challenges to their authority.

Otherwise, evidence of subgroup discrimination—when domestic political structures openly discriminate against certain social, ethnic, racial, or political groups—is associated with regime-led violence. This is not all that surprising since brazen political, economic, or social discrimination is an intuitive precursor to outright mass violence.

Countries with larger populations and a recent history of coup attempts (either in-country or in surrounding countries) similarly tend to experience mass killings at a higher rate. The effect of recent coups on mass killings is particularly interesting as some coups, such as the 1991 coup in Moscow or the 2015 coup in Burkina Faso, triggered nonviolent mobilizations that defeated the putschists, arguably preventing greater bloodshed than had the coup leaders been challenged with arms. Elsewhere coups were preceded by nonviolent uprisings such as in Egypt, where the Tamarod campaign in May and June of 2013 paved the way for the Egyptian military to issue an ultimatum and oust President Morsi from office in July. This, however, was then followed by mass killings of supporters of President Morsi and the Muslim Brotherhood who organized to protest the coup.[13]

Perhaps not surprisingly, we also find that one of the best predictors of mass killings are evidence of recent mass killings. In other words, countries that have ordered a mass killing in the last five years are much more likely to do so again. It could be that these countries have already broken the taboo against mass violence which leaves them with few reasons to refrain from doing so again. For instance, consider the case of Syria where the international community has already condemned Bashar Al-Assad for killing his own civilians. Having successfully weathered these condemnations, and realizing the international community is perhaps unwilling to intervene directly, there is little preventing Assad from using violence again. Moreover, countries that have already mobilized and successfully utilized their domestic forces for mass violence have reduced uncertainty over whether their troops will be willing to kill again if given the order to do so. This uncertainty, however, might be a key reason why leaders refrain from mass killings in the first place.

Box 3: Mass killings in Biafra

The Nigerian Civil War erupted several years after Nigeria gained independence from the United Kingdom in 1960. The war followed a tumultuous period of repeated coups, widespread political corruption, and ethnic discrimination and violence against the Igbo population—structural factors that are all widely associated with governmental violence. Yet what seems to have triggered mass killings was the eastern region of Nigeria declaring its independence, naming itself the Republic of Biafra. Biafran and Nigerian forces waged numerous battles near the border of the newly formed Republic. Then, after a period of stalemate, Nigerian forces besieged Biafra, causing widespread deaths as a result of famine and disease. The Nigerian armed forces were also directed to kill Biafran civilians. In one incident alone, they were reported to have slain at least 1,000 individuals in the city of Asaba. Though exact numbers are difficult to come by, some estimate that more than 500,000 civilian noncombatants were eventually killed.

Sources: Bird, S. Elizabeth, and Fraser Ottanelli. "The Asaba massacre and the Nigerian civil war: reclaiming hidden history." *Journal of Genocide Research* 16.2-3 (2014): 379-399.

Valentino, Benjamin A. "Final solutions: Mass killing and genocide in the 20th century." Cornell University Press, 2003.

II. Campaign-level factors: nonviolent discipline; campaigns' goals; defections; external assistance

In addition to the structural conditions identified above, we find that campaign dynamics also shape the odds of mass killings. This includes:

1. Whether dissidents remain primarily nonviolent;
2. The goals of the opposition campaign;
3. The behavior of the military during the conflict; and
4. The degree of external involvement in the uprising.

Perhaps most significantly, we find that uprisings that remain steadfastly nonviolent experience a likelihood of mass atrocities that is three times lower than violent resistance, holding their goals and other factors constant.

Moreover, the violence-dampening effect of nonviolent mobilization is amplified when protesters can encourage military defections. Nonviolent movements that manage to elicit defections from the armed forces tend to reduce the odds of mass violence from the regime by as much as 88%. This result echoes findings in the literature on strategic nonviolent conflict, where "political jiujitsu" and forging links between activists and soldiers are advocated as ways to sew cracks in the regime and prevent violent suppression.[14]

With regard to dissidents' goals, we find that campaigns aimed at removing the incumbent leadership—compared to campaigns seeking territorial goals[15]—are much more likely to encounter mass killings. Specifically, the threat of mass atrocities is over 10 times greater. However, even in struggles where the dissidents are attempting to overthrow the government, nonviolent resistance still has a lower expected odds of mass killings than does violent rebellion.

Regarding external involvement, states are nearly 25 times more likely to crack down on civilians when only the dissident campaign receives foreign state support; 5 times more likely when only the regime receives support; and 21 times more likely when both the state and the campaign have foreign backing. This effect holds true regardless of whether that campaign is violent or nonviolent. Therefore, any form of foreign state support, either to the state or to the dissident campaign, can increase the likelihood of mass killings, even in the case of a nonviolent movement.

Taken together, these findings regarding campaign-level factors suggest a counterintuitive paradox: that dissidents who remain unarmed and maintain an indigenous support base are at a lower risk of provoking widespread civilian victimization than those who take up arms and/or seek outside support to protect themselves against state abuses. Rather than seeking to challenge the regime head-on through violent mobilization backed by powerful foreign allies, dissidents might be safer with alternative strategies that internalize nonviolent discipline, reflected in activists' peaceful actions and grassroots mobilization—especially in the face of their opponent's violence.

Ultimately, these findings provide policymakers and concerned citizens with greater insight into the timing of mass atrocities. Information on when uprisings begin and how they are organized can help onlookers anticipate imminent mass violence. In contrast, slow-moving structural indicators might suggest that violence is perhaps more likely, but it may remain likely for the next decade or the entire duration of a particular regime. While the latter provides little actionable information, the campaign dynamics unfolding in real time offer immediate avenues for preventive or ameliorating actions. This topic is further explored in Key Takeaways at the end of this report.

> # Box 4: Civil resistance in Serbia
>
> In September of 2000, citizens of Yugoslavia took to the polls and handed a defeat to the incumbent leader, Slobodan Milosevic. To the surprise of many, however, federal authorities declared that no candidate had received more than 50% of the vote. While this triggered a runoff election, it also led to widespread accusations of vote tampering and electoral fraud. Protesters, supported by the student-led Otpor movement, soon organized to contest the election with one of the first acts of nonviolent resistance being led by miners in the Kolubara district. Momentum continued to build until October 5, 2000, when several hundred thousand activists descended on Belgrade to demand that Milosevic step down.
>
> Although this conflict exhibits many of the structural factors conducive to mass killings—an entrenched autocratic ruler with a history of mass-civilian victimization, a regime immersed in civil wars for almost a decade and persistent subgroup discrimination—members of the police and armed forces refused to fire on activists despite orders to do so. As to why, they often noted that they could not bring themselves to use force because the nonviolent protesters—their fellow citizens—posed little threat. This was precisely the goal of Otpor strategists who years before had come face to face with government repression. They concluded that driving a wedge between state leaders and their security forces was critical to success, and that remaining steadfastly nonviolent, combined with deliberate outreach to and fraternization with the police and the military, would be critical to remaining safe. Ultimately, the activists successfully avoided mass atrocities despite structural indicators that suggested a high likelihood of violent confrontations.
>
> Source: Binnendijk, Anika Locke, and Ivan Marovic. "Power and persuasion: Nonviolent strategies to influence state security forces in Serbia (2000) and Ukraine (2004)." *Communist and Post-Communist Studies* 39.3 (2006): 411-42.

III. Assessing campaign and structural factors: which matter more?

To assess whether campaign or structural factors are more influential, we ranked each variable in our analysis according to its relative impact on our ability to predict mass killings in the out-of-sample validation exercise.[16]

The table on the next page demonstrates that a mix of structural and campaign-level factors is important, implying that both must be taken into account when assessing the risk of mass violence. For structural variables, we find that regime type, population, subgroup discrimination, and coups matter most; for campaign factors, goals, method of resistance, and defections are most influential. Straddling these two categories are recent mass killings (whether one occurred in the previous five years) and the total number of simultaneous uprisings in a country.

Top 10 predictors impacting odds of mass killings

- Recent mass killing +
- Party regime +
- External support to campaign only +
- Goal: Government overthrow +
- Population +
- Coup attempt, past five years −
- Military regime +
- Subgroup discrimination +
- Nonviolent campaign with military defections −
- Multiple, concurrent resistance campaigns +

Note: +/− indicate the variable's impact on the likelihood of mass killings. Variables listed in order of their impact on predictive power.

> ## Box 5: Mass killings in Syria and the evolving campaign of resistance
>
> The ongoing Syrian civil war can be traced back to initially nonviolent protests that began in March 2011 in the southern city of Deraa. Protests soon spread throughout the country and the Assad regime was quick to crack down, using imprisonment, torture, and violence against those involved. Faced with this turn of events, protesters largely abandoned nonviolent tactics to take up arms in a bid to overthrow the regime. Mass killings in Syria began almost immediately: reports suggest that 2,019 individuals were killed between March and August of 2011, even while the movement was primarily nonviolent. The next five months witnessed a significant increase of up to 3,144 deaths, that more than doubled to 8,195 deaths in the subsequent five months from January to June of 2012 when predominantly violent tactics were embraced by both sides.
>
> Structural explanations would suggest that Syria was ripe for mass atrocities: the country is governed by a long-standing, personalist regime that has long relied on the military for support, and there has been evidence of institutionalized discrimination against the Kurds and others. While some campaign-level factors such as a nonviolent discipline show a lower likelihood of mass killings (an initial nonviolent phase on the part of the movement), others are indeed associated with state-led violence (eventual insurgency, multiple ongoing campaigns, foreign support, and goals of regime overthrow).
>
> Source: Bartkowski, Maciej, and Mohja Kahf. "The Syrian resistance: a tale of two struggles, Part 2." *opendemocracy.net*, September 24, 2013.
>
> "Syria, events of 2009." *Human Rights Watch*. https://www.hrw.org/world-report/2010/country-chapters/syria.

Key takeaways

Our research shows that structural variables associated with mass killings are in general relatively static and not easily alterable—especially in short term—either by domestic dissidents or outside actors. This includes, among others: regime type, poverty, subgroup discrimination, and the number of coups. Yet, there are other factors that either dissidents or outside forces can indeed influence to help prevent mass violence, including:

- The campaign's strategic choices: Maintaining nonviolent discipline despite regime provocations;
- Not soliciting support from external states;
- Isolating the incumbent regime;
- Coordinating and eliciting defections among security forces.

Ultimately, the findings in this report underscore the meaningful impact that campaign-level factors have on the likelihood of mass killings—factors that have been previously ignored and that can be altered, augmented, or avoided by the actors themselves. As such, our results have important implications for dissidents, policymakers, and other concerned groups.

For dissidents: Insights on how to lower the risk of mass killings

For activists seeking to challenge the regime while reducing the likelihood of mass atrocities, our research suggests that choices to maintain nonviolent discipline are key, especially when confronting brutal, committed regimes. Although it is the case that nonviolent uprisings often face beatings, arrest, and other forms of coercion including some isolated incidents of lethal violence, violent uprisings are correlated with a much greater risk of large-scale civilian victimization—specifically, they are more than three times as likely to experience mass violence. Choices by resisters about whether or not to actively seek direct international aid are also important. Our findings ultimately suggest that foreign material assistance to an uprising, whether violent or nonviolent, can work to dissidents' disadvantage. By collaborating with foreign states, the movement might appear increasingly threatening to regime elites and their security forces. Although we cannot say for sure, other forms of external assistance may prove more useful. n Argentina and East Timor, for instance, foreign states supported the opposition not by sending money or arms, but by bringing attention to atrocities committed by the regime. Ultimately, more research is needed to better understand how various foreign actors—including states, NGOs, and diasporas—and different types of external assistance can support popular uprisings and prevent mass atrocities.

Therefore, dissidents should view with caution any attempts from foreign states to provide them with direct support (e.g. material or financial assistance) and should instead seek outside assistance on a selective basis where it helps to address specific needs or weaknesses (e.g. its capacity to manage repression or to enhance its tactical innovation). Another, perhaps safer way to leverage outside support is in the form of less tangible and less visible knowledge sharing and strategy honing rather than direct assistance. This type of support and actions that can be offered by external state and non-state actors could include:

- Providing dissidents with information on organizing and maintaining nonviolent discipline that can also limit the likelihood of regime retribution; and
- Devising effective strategies for encouraging defections from and noncooperation by the armed forces.

Though maintaining nonviolent discipline is useful in this regard,[17] campaigners should also consider, where possible, developing and deploying a wide range of nonviolent tactics to facilitate defections, including:

- Appealing to their shared interests and backgrounds;
- Relying on retired army officers to reach out to their serving colleagues;
- Offering assistance and solidarity to those who defect and their families;
- Encouraging different types of loyalty shifts, including deliberate inefficiency in implementing orders rather than outright defections; and
- Suggesting that officers demand written orders from their superiors if asked to engage in killings, among others.

Ultimately, if regime elites cannot count on the support of their armed forces, then they are less likely to risk widespread defection by ordering them to kill their fellow citizens.

Finally, campaigns and individual dissidents can collect information that might be useful for preventing mass atrocities in the future. There is a need for activists as well as domestic and international actors on the ground to meticulously record and collect relevant information including evidence of when, how and in what way nonviolent mobilization and self-organization might have protected communities and reduced their exposure to mass violence. This data, in turn, would help both future dissidents and external actors to develop more effective policy instruments to prevent mass atrocities.

For foreign states, policymakers, and NGOs: How to support nonviolent movements while preventing mass killings

The focus on campaign-level factors, including assistance to nonviolent movements, provide viable short and medium-term strategies to prevent violence. This lies in stark contrast to strategies geared toward the structural causes of mass violence that require long-term commitments by policy makers to help develop democratic institutions and grow underdeveloped economies.

In the short term, external actors interested in reducing the prevalence of mass violence have several options available to them. They can use their influence to steer uprisings toward strategies, actions, and dynamics that are associated with a lower odds of mass violence. To begin with, we find that overt support for foreign uprisings as well as foreign regimes raises the likelihood of mass killings. Regimes may feel particularly threatened when facing a foreign-backed adversary, whereas foreign support for a regime may convince it that it is justified in its actions, no matter how violent it may become. If, however, foreign actors are determined to get involved, then support based on political, diplomatic, or knowledge and skills-sharing—rather than direct financial or material assistance—might be the safest approach.[18]

Additionally, since violent uprisings are more likely to experience mass killings, states could use their leverage to pressure movements into remaining nonviolent. Political support and diplomatic engagement, for instance, could be conditional upon the opposition movement foregoing acts of violence. When movements do remain nonviolent, states can then issue statements of public solidarity as well. The benefits of this are twofold: While we find that nonviolent movements are generally safer, other research suggests that such movements are more likely to succeed as well.[19] Moreover, expressions of solidarity may be less likely to elicit backlash against the movement (as opposed to direct material assistance by states). Last, since we find that military defections are negatively correlated with the odds of mass violence, states could take steps to undermine the cohesion of foreign regimes and their armed forces. Offering exile to military leaders, for example, and setting up a permanent fund to help relocate defectors and their families might encourage military officials to more seriously consider a potential exit. And, if regime leaders are aware that their security forces have more opportunities and incentives (provided by external actors) for disobedience and defection, they might be increasingly hesitant to order an unpopular crackdown in the first place. Similarly, states could establish military-to-military contacts with foreign allies to promote democratic values and respect nonviolent protesters.[20] Then, when regime-led violence does appear imminent, condemnations, targeted sanctions, and other measures that send clear signals of disapproval might also be effective.

In the long term, states can promote policies that take aim at the structural roots of mass violence. Specifically, states can work to reduce subgroup discrimination, bolster democratic institutions, and encourage economic development. Although these actions will take place over the course of years or decades, they should lower the likelihood of mass atrocities in the long run. What might be most effective, however, is a combination of both campaign-focused and structural approaches. States and the international development community should maintain their focus on reducing poverty and discrimination while cultivating democracy. At the same time, they should consider working with specialized civil society groups to closely monitor uprisings and look for ways to make them safer.

Future research

Investigations into why mass atrocities occur help us understand when and where such events are likely to take place. Future research on this topic should therefore continue to employ holistic approaches that recognize the diverse array of factors contributing to mass violence. This would include characteristics of uprisings that challenge repressive authorities as well as foundational structural variables that capture the conditions inside countries at particular points in time. Additionally, more research that further disaggregates campaign-level variables can help activists, policymakers, and other actors stay fully informed when searching for solutions to prevent mass atrocities.

End Notes

[1] Data on mass killings comes from the State-Led Mass Killing Episode data set (Ulfelder and Valentino 2010). See https://github.com/ulfelder/earlywarningproject-statrisk-2014/blob/master/masskillling.data.handbook.txt.

[2] Episodes of Contention (MEC) project. Available at: https://www.du.edu/korbel/sie/research/chenow_mec_major_episodes_contention-1.html.

[3] Pinckney, Jonathan. *Making or Breaking Nonviolent Discipline in Civil Resistance Movements*. ICNC Monograph Series. Washington, DC: ICNC Press, 2016. https://www.nonviolent-conflict.org/explaining-nonviolent-discipline-civil-resistance-struggles/.

[4] Hill, Daniel W., Jr., and Zachary M. Jones. 2014. An empirical evaluation of explanations for state repression. *American Political Science Review* 108(3): 661–687; Davenport, Christian. 2007. State repression and political order. *Annual Review of Political Science* 10:1-23. Valentino, Benjamin. 2004. *Final solutions: Genocide and mass killings in the 20th century*. Ithaca, NY: Cornell University Press; Valentino, Benjamin, Paul Huth, and Dylan Balch-Lindsay. 2004. Draining the sea: Mass killing and guerrilla warfare. *International Organization* 58, no. 2 (May): 375-407. Kalyvas, Stathis. 2006. *The logic of violence in civil war*. New York: Cambridge University Press. Davenport, Christian D. 2008. *State repression and the domestic democratic peace*. New York: Cambridge University Press. Ulfelder, Jay and Valentino, Benjamin, "Assessing Risks of State-Sponsored Mass Killing" (February 1, 2008). Available at SSRN: https://ssrn.com/abstract=1703426. Young, Joseph K. "Repression, dissent, and the onset of civil war." *Political Research Quarterly* 66.3 (2013): 516-532. Carey, Sabine C. "The use of repression as a response to domestic dissent." *Political Studies* 58.1 (2010): 167-186.

[5] Importantly, while nonviolent campaigns might pose a greater threat to the survival of the regime (as recent research suggests) such movements are less likely to personally threaten regime elites, their families, and their supporters.

[6] Valentino, Benjamin, Paul Huth, and Dylan Balch-Lindsay. "'Draining the sea': mass killing and guerrilla warfare." *International Organization* 58.2 (2004): 375-407.

[7] Valentino, Benjamin A. *Final solutions: Mass killing and genocide in the 20th century*.

    Cornell University Press, 2003.

[8] To study how campaign and structural factors interact to influence the occurrence of mass killings, we analyze data from 1955-2013 on the occurrence of mass killings across the globe. Data for these analyses is pulled from a variety of datasets including Major Episodes of Contention (MEC), Polity, Archigos, World Development Indicators, and Ulfelder and Valentino (for mass killings; see endnote 1). We are, unfortunately, presently limited to studying mass atrocities through 2013 due to the availability of existing data.

[9] This research extends—but is not identical to—research we conducted as part of the Political Instability Task Force in support of President Obama's Atrocities Prevention Board in 2014-2015. More information on our methodology can be found in our working paper, available at: https://papers.ssrn.com/sol3/papers.cfm?abstract_id=3045189.

[10] While the 2000-2013 period gives us a large enough sample to work with, it also focuses our predictions on some of the most recent mass atrocities that are likely to exhibit similar dynamics to those occurring in the near future. Then, by continually refining our models to improve our predictions, we can hone in on the factors that ultimately give us the most predictive power. For more on prediction and correlational analysis, see: Ward, Michael D., Brian D. Greenhill, and Kristin M. Bakke. "The perils of policy by p value: Predicting civil conflicts." *Journal of Peace Research* 47.4 (2010): 363-375.

[11] To be sure, while the benefits of out-of-sample validation are many, it cannot overcome the fact that we are limited to observational data. While prediction—compared to simple correlation—is more useful for understanding the factors that precede or are contemporaneous to mass killings, one must be cautious not to infer causality from our results.

[12] It is important to note that many of these factors are included to account for the possibility that nonviolent movements take place in more lenient conditions, leading to the lower observed rate of mass killings. While we cannot fully rule this out here, relegated research suggests this is not the case. For example, see: Chenoweth, Erica, and Jay Ulfelder. "Can structural conditions explain the onset of nonviolent uprisings?" *Journal of Conflict Resolution* 61.2 (2017): 298-324.

[13] Zunes, Stephen. *Civil Resistance Against Coups: A Comparative and Historical*

[13] *Perspective*. ICNC Monograph Series. Washington, DC: ICNC Press, 2017. https://www.nonviolent-conflict.org/civil-resistance-against-coups/.

[14] Sharp, Gene. *The Politics of Nonviolent Action*. Vol. 3. Boston: P. Sargent Publisher, 1973.

[15] The full list of reference categories is included in our working paper available at https://papers.ssrn.com/sol3/papers.cfm?abstract_id=3045189.

[16] This process relies on stepwise variable deletion from the full predictive model. After deleting one variable at a time, we reassess the model's predictive performance using out-of-sample validation. We then measure whether the model's performance is better or worse, and we can subsequently rank variables by their relative impact.

[17] Chenoweth, Erica, and Maria J. Stephan. *Why Civil Resistance Works: The Strategic Logic of Nonviolent Conflict*. Columbia University Press, 2011.

[18] No matter the type of assistance, it might be best to take steps to limit the visibility of the cooperation. However, more research is needed on this topic.

[19] Chenoweth, Erica, and Maria J. Stephan. *Why Civil Resistance Works: The Strategic Logic of Nonviolent Conflict*. Columbia University Press, 2011.

[20] Blair, Dennis C., ed. *Military Engagement: Influencing Armed Forces Worldwide to Support Democratic Transitions*. Vol. 2. Brookings Institution Press, 2013.

www.ingramcontent.com/pod-product-compliance
Lightning Source LLC
Chambersburg PA
CBHW040225040426
42333CB00054B/3453